THE
Podcast Plan

for your first 90 episodes

THE
Podcast Plan
for your first 90 episodes

Pre-Show
Checklist

Checklist:

_____

_____

_____

_____

_____

_____

_____

_____

_____

_____

_____

Notes

Post-Show Checklist

_____

_____

_____

_____

_____

_____

_____

_____

_____

_____

_____

_____

Notes

Notes

Episode Details

Title:

Episode #:

Recording Date: Release Date:

HOSTS	GUESTS
☐ _____	_____
☐ _____	_____
☐ _____	_____

Discussion Topics

☐ _____

☐ _____

☐ _____

☐ _____

☐ _____

☐ _____

☐ _____

Intentions & Goals

_____

_____

_____

_____

Notes

_____

_____

_____

_____

_____

_____

_____

_____

_____

_____

Show Rating: ☆☆☆☆☆

Episode Details

Title:

Episode #:

Recording Date: Release Date:

HOSTS	GUESTS

Discussion Topics

Intentions & Goals

_____

_____

_____

_____

Notes

_____

_____

_____

_____

_____

_____

_____

_____

_____

_____

_____

_____

Show Rating: ☆☆☆☆☆

Episode Details

Title:

Episode #:

Recording Date: Release Date:

HOSTS	GUESTS
☐ _____	_____
☐ _____	_____
☐ _____	_____

Discussion Topics

☐ _____

☐ _____

☐ _____

☐ _____

☐ _____

☐ _____

☐ _____

Intentions & Goals

_____

_____

_____

_____

Notes

_____

_____

_____

_____

_____

_____

_____

_____

_____

_____

_____

Show Rating: ☆☆☆☆☆

Episode Details

Title:

Episode #:

Recording Date: Release Date:

HOSTS	GUESTS

Discussion Topics

Intentions & Goals

_____

_____

_____

_____

Notes

_____

_____

_____

_____

_____

_____

_____

_____

_____

_____

_____

_____

_____

_____

Show Rating: ☆☆☆☆☆

Episode Details

Title:

Episode #:

Recording Date: Release Date:

HOSTS	GUESTS

Discussion Topics

Intentions & Goals

_____

_____

_____

_____

Notes

_____

_____

_____

_____

_____

_____

_____

_____

_____

_____

_____

_____

Show Rating: ☆☆☆☆☆

Episode Details

Title:

Episode #:

Recording Date: Release Date:

HOSTS	GUESTS

Discussion Topics

Intentions & Goals

_____

_____

_____

_____

Notes

_____

_____

_____

_____

_____

_____

_____

_____

_____

_____

_____

_____

_____

Show Rating: ☆☆☆☆☆

Episode Details

Title:

Episode #:

Recording Date: Release Date:

HOSTS	GUESTS

Discussion Topics

Intentions & Goals

_____

_____

_____

_____

Notes

_____

_____

_____

_____

_____

_____

_____

_____

_____

_____

_____

Show Rating: ☆☆☆☆☆

Episode Details

Title:

Episode #:

Recording Date: Release Date:

HOSTS	GUESTS

Discussion Topics

Intentions & Goals

_____

_____

_____

_____

Notes

_____

_____

_____

_____

_____

_____

_____

_____

_____

_____

_____

Show Rating: ☆☆☆☆☆

Episode Details

Title:

Episode #:

Recording Date: Release Date:

HOSTS	GUESTS

Discussion Topics

Intentions & Goals

_____

_____

_____

_____

Notes

_____

_____

_____

_____

_____

_____

_____

_____

_____

_____

_____

_____

_____

Show Rating: ☆☆☆☆☆

Episode Details

Title:

Episode #:

Recording Date: Release Date:

HOSTS	GUESTS

Discussion Topics

Intentions & Goals

Notes

Show Rating: ☆☆☆☆☆

Episode Details

Title:

Episode #:

Recording Date: Release Date:

HOSTS	GUESTS

Discussion Topics

Intentions & Goals

_____

_____

_____

_____

Notes

_____

_____

_____

_____

_____

_____

_____

_____

_____

_____

_____

_____

Show Rating: ☆☆☆☆☆

Episode Details

Title:

Episode #:

Recording Date: Release Date:

HOSTS	GUESTS
☐ _____	_____
☐ _____	_____
☐ _____	_____

Discussion Topics

- ☐ _____
- ☐ _____
- ☐ _____
- ☐ _____
- ☐ _____
- ☐ _____
- ☐ _____

Intentions & Goals

_____

_____

_____

_____

Notes

_____

_____

_____

_____

_____

_____

_____

_____

_____

_____

_____

Show Rating: ☆☆☆☆☆

Episode Details

Title:

Episode #:

Recording Date: Release Date:

HOSTS	GUESTS

Discussion Topics

Intentions & Goals

_____
_____
_____
_____

Notes

_____
_____
_____
_____
_____
_____
_____
_____
_____
_____
_____

Show Rating: ☆☆☆☆☆

Episode Details

Title:

Episode #:

Recording Date: Release Date:

HOSTS	GUESTS
☐ _____	_____
☐ _____	_____
☐ _____	_____

Discussion Topics

- ☐ _____
- ☐ _____
- ☐ _____
- ☐ _____
- ☐ _____
- ☐ _____
- ☐ _____

Intentions & Goals

_____

_____

_____

_____

Notes

_____

_____

_____

_____

_____

_____

_____

_____

_____

_____

_____

Show Rating: ☆☆☆☆☆

Episode Details

Title:

Episode #:

Recording Date: Release Date:

HOSTS	GUESTS

Discussion Topics

Intentions & Goals

Notes

Show Rating: ☆☆☆☆☆

Episode Details

Title:

Episode #:

Recording Date: Release Date:

HOSTS	GUESTS
☐ _____	_____
☐ _____	_____
☐ _____	_____

Discussion Topics

☐ _____

☐ _____

☐ _____

☐ _____

☐ _____

☐ _____

☐ _____

Intentions & Goals

_____

_____

_____

_____

Notes

_____

_____

_____

_____

_____

_____

_____

_____

_____

_____

_____

_____

Show Rating: ☆☆☆☆☆

Episode Details

Title:

Episode #:

Recording Date: Release Date:

HOSTS	GUESTS

Discussion Topics

Intentions & Goals

Notes

Show Rating: ☆☆☆☆☆

Episode Details

Title:

Episode #:

Recording Date: Release Date:

HOSTS	GUESTS

Discussion Topics

Intentions & Goals

_____

_____

_____

Notes

_____

_____

_____

_____

_____

_____

_____

_____

_____

_____

Show Rating: ☆☆☆☆☆

Episode Details

Title:

Episode #:

Recording Date: Release Date:

HOSTS	GUESTS

Discussion Topics

Intentions & Goals

Notes

Show Rating: ☆☆☆☆☆

Episode Details

Title:

Episode #:

Recording Date: Release Date:

HOSTS	GUESTS

Discussion Topics

Intentions & Goals

_____

_____

_____

_____

Notes

_____

_____

_____

_____

_____

_____

_____

_____

_____

_____

_____

_____

_____

Show Rating: ☆☆☆☆☆

Episode Details

Title:

Episode #:

Recording Date: Release Date:

HOSTS	GUESTS

Discussion Topics

Intentions & Goals

_____

_____

_____

_____

Notes

_____

_____

_____

_____

_____

_____

_____

_____

_____

_____

_____

_____

Show Rating: ☆☆☆☆☆

Episode Details

Title:

Episode #:

Recording Date: Release Date:

HOSTS	GUESTS

Discussion Topics

Intentions & Goals

_____

_____

_____

_____

Notes

_____

_____

_____

_____

_____

_____

_____

_____

_____

_____

_____

Show Rating: ☆☆☆☆☆

Episode Details

Title:

Episode #:

Recording Date:

Release Date:

HOSTS	GUESTS

- [ ] _____
- [ ] _____
- [ ] _____

Discussion Topics

- [ ] _____
- [ ] _____
- [ ] _____
- [ ] _____
- [ ] _____
- [ ] _____
- [ ] _____

Intentions & Goals

_____

_____

_____

_____

Notes

_____

_____

_____

_____

_____

_____

_____

_____

_____

_____

_____

Show Rating: ☆☆☆☆☆

Episode Details

Title:

Episode #:

Recording Date: Release Date:

HOSTS	GUESTS

Discussion Topics

Intentions & Goals

Notes

Show Rating: ☆☆☆☆☆

Episode Details

Title:

Episode #:

Recording Date: Release Date:

HOSTS	GUESTS

Discussion Topics

Intentions & Goals

_____

_____

_____

_____

Notes

_____

_____

_____

_____

_____

_____

_____

_____

_____

_____

Show Rating: ☆☆☆☆☆

Episode Details

Title:

Episode #:

Recording Date: Release Date:

HOSTS	GUESTS

- ☐ _____
- ☐ _____
- ☐ _____

_____
_____
_____

Discussion Topics

- ☐ _____
- ☐ _____
- ☐ _____
- ☐ _____
- ☐ _____
- ☐ _____
- ☐ _____

Intentions & Goals

_____

_____

_____

_____

Notes

_____

_____

_____

_____

_____

_____

_____

_____

_____

_____

_____

Show Rating: ☆☆☆☆☆

Episode Details

Title:

Episode #:

Recording Date: Release Date:

HOSTS	GUESTS

Discussion Topics

Intentions & Goals

_____

_____

_____

_____

Notes

_____

_____

_____

_____

_____

_____

_____

_____

_____

_____

_____

Show Rating: ☆☆☆☆☆

Episode Details

Title:

Episode #:

Recording Date: Release Date:

HOSTS	GUESTS

Discussion Topics

Intentions & Goals

_____

_____

_____

_____

Notes

_____

_____

_____

_____

_____

_____

_____

_____

_____

_____

Show Rating: ☆☆☆☆☆

Episode Details

Title:

Episode #:

Recording Date: Release Date:

HOSTS	GUESTS
☐ _____	_____
☐ _____	_____
☐ _____	_____

Discussion Topics

☐ _____

☐ _____

☐ _____

☐ _____

☐ _____

☐ _____

☐ _____

Intentions & Goals

_____

_____

_____

_____

Notes

_____

_____

_____

_____

_____

_____

_____

_____

_____

_____

_____

Show Rating: ☆☆☆☆☆

Episode Details

Title:

Episode #:

Recording Date: Release Date:

HOSTS	GUESTS

Discussion Topics

Intentions & Goals

Notes

Show Rating: ☆☆☆☆☆

Episode Details

Title:

Episode #:

Recording Date: Release Date:

HOSTS	GUESTS

Discussion Topics

Intentions & Goals

Notes

Show Rating: ☆☆☆☆☆

Episode Details

Title:

Episode #:

Recording Date: Release Date:

HOSTS	GUESTS
☐ _____	_____
☐ _____	_____
☐ _____	_____

Discussion Topics

☐ _____

☐ _____

☐ _____

☐ _____

☐ _____

☐ _____

☐ _____

Intentions & Goals

_____

_____

_____

_____

Notes

_____

_____

_____

_____

_____

_____

_____

_____

_____

_____

_____

Show Rating: ☆☆☆☆☆

Episode Details

Title:

Episode #:

Recording Date: Release Date:

HOSTS	GUESTS
☐ _____	_____
☐ _____	_____
☐ _____	_____

Discussion Topics

☐ _____

☐ _____

☐ _____

☐ _____

☐ _____

☐ _____

☐ _____

Intentions & Goals

Notes

Show Rating: ☆☆☆☆☆

Episode Details

Title:

Episode #:

Recording Date: Release Date:

HOSTS	GUESTS
☐ _____	_____
☐ _____	_____
☐ _____	_____

Discussion Topics

☐ _____

☐ _____

☐ _____

☐ _____

☐ _____

☐ _____

☐ _____

Intentions & Goals

_____

_____

_____

_____

Notes

_____

_____

_____

_____

_____

_____

_____

_____

_____

_____

_____

_____

Show Rating: ☆ ☆ ☆ ☆ ☆

Episode Details

Title:

Episode #:

Recording Date:

Release Date:

HOSTS	GUESTS

Discussion Topics

Intentions & Goals

Notes

Show Rating: ☆☆☆☆☆

Episode Details

Title:

Episode #:

Recording Date: Release Date:

HOSTS	GUESTS

Discussion Topics

Intentions & Goals

_____

_____

_____

_____

Notes

_____

_____

_____

_____

_____

_____

_____

_____

_____

_____

_____

_____

Show Rating: ☆☆☆☆☆

Episode Details

Title:

Episode #:

Recording Date: Release Date:

HOSTS	GUESTS

Discussion Topics

Intentions & Goals

_____

_____

_____

_____

Notes

_____

_____

_____

_____

_____

_____

_____

_____

_____

_____

_____

Show Rating: ☆☆☆☆☆

Episode Details

Title:

Episode #:

Recording Date:

Release Date:

HOSTS	GUESTS

Discussion Topics

Intentions & Goals

_____

_____

_____

Notes

_____

_____

_____

_____

_____

_____

_____

_____

_____

_____

Show Rating: ☆☆☆☆☆

Episode Details

Title:

Episode #:

Recording Date: Release Date:

HOSTS	GUESTS
☐ _____	_____
☐ _____	_____
☐ _____	_____

Discussion Topics

☐ _____

☐ _____

☐ _____

☐ _____

☐ _____

☐ _____

☐ _____

Intentions & Goals

Notes

Show Rating: ☆ ☆ ☆ ☆ ☆

Episode Details

Title:

Episode #:

Recording Date: Release Date:

HOSTS	GUESTS

Discussion Topics

Intentions & Goals

Notes

Show Rating: ☆☆☆☆☆

Episode Details

Title:

Episode #:

Recording Date: Release Date:

HOSTS	GUESTS

Discussion Topics

Intentions & Goals

_____

_____

_____

Notes

_____

_____

_____

_____

_____

_____

_____

_____

_____

_____

Show Rating: ☆☆☆☆☆

Episode Details

Title:

Episode #:

Recording Date: Release Date:

HOSTS	GUESTS

Discussion Topics

Intentions & Goals

Notes

Show Rating: ☆☆☆☆☆

Episode Details

Title:

Episode #:

Recording Date: Release Date:

HOSTS	GUESTS
☐ _____	_____
☐ _____	_____
☐ _____	_____

Discussion Topics

☐ _____

☐ _____

☐ _____

☐ _____

☐ _____

☐ _____

☐ _____

Intentions & Goals

Notes

Show Rating: ☆☆☆☆☆

Episode Details

Title:

Episode #:

Recording Date: Release Date:

HOSTS	GUESTS

Discussion Topics

Intentions & Goals

Notes

Show Rating: ☆ ☆ ☆ ☆ ☆

Episode Details

Title:

Episode #:

Recording Date: Release Date:

HOSTS	GUESTS
☐ _____	_____
☐ _____	_____
☐ _____	_____

Discussion Topics

☐ _____

☐ _____

☐ _____

☐ _____

☐ _____

☐ _____

☐ _____

Intentions & Goals

Notes

Show Rating: ☆☆☆☆☆

Episode Details

Title:

Episode #:

Recording Date:

Release Date:

HOSTS	GUESTS
☐	
☐	
☐	

Discussion Topics

☐

☐

☐

☐

☐

☐

☐

Intentions & Goals

_____

_____

_____

Notes

_____

_____

_____

_____

_____

_____

_____

_____

_____

_____

_____

Show Rating: ☆☆☆☆☆

Episode Details

Title:

Episode #:

Recording Date: Release Date:

HOSTS	GUESTS

Discussion Topics

Intentions & Goals

_____

_____

_____

_____

Notes

_____

_____

_____

_____

_____

_____

_____

_____

_____

_____

_____

Show Rating: ☆☆☆☆☆

Episode Details

Title:

Episode #:

Recording Date: Release Date:

HOSTS	GUESTS

Discussion Topics

Intentions & Goals

Notes

Show Rating: ☆☆☆☆☆

Episode Details

Title:

Episode #:

Recording Date: Release Date:

HOSTS	GUESTS
☐ _____	_____
☐ _____	_____
☐ _____	_____

Discussion Topics

☐ _____

☐ _____

☐ _____

☐ _____

☐ _____

☐ _____

☐ _____

Intentions & Goals

_____

_____

_____

Notes

_____

_____

_____

_____

_____

_____

_____

_____

_____

_____

_____

Show Rating: ☆☆☆☆☆

Episode Details

Title:

Episode #:

Recording Date: Release Date:

HOSTS	GUESTS
☐	
☐	
☐	

Discussion Topics

- ☐
- ☐
- ☐
- ☐
- ☐
- ☐
- ☐

Intentions & Goals

_____

_____

_____

_____

Notes

_____

_____

_____

_____

_____

_____

_____

_____

_____

_____

Show Rating: ☆ ☆ ☆ ☆ ☆

Episode Details

Title:

Episode #:

Recording Date: Release Date:

HOSTS	GUESTS
☐ _____	_____
☐ _____	_____
☐ _____	_____

Discussion Topics

☐ _____

☐ _____

☐ _____

☐ _____

☐ _____

☐ _____

☐ _____

Intentions & Goals

_____
_____
_____
_____

Notes

_____
_____
_____
_____
_____
_____
_____
_____
_____
_____
_____

Show Rating: ☆☆☆☆☆

Episode Details

Title:

Episode #:

Recording Date: Release Date:

HOSTS	GUESTS

☐ _____   _____

☐ _____   _____

☐ _____   _____

Discussion Topics

☐ _____

☐ _____

☐ _____

☐ _____

☐ _____

☐ _____

☐ _____

Intentions & Goals

_____

_____

_____

_____

Notes

_____

_____

_____

_____

_____

_____

_____

_____

_____

_____

_____

_____

_____

Show Rating: ☆☆☆☆☆

Episode Details

Title:

Episode #:

Recording Date: Release Date:

HOSTS	GUESTS
☐ _____	_____
☐ _____	_____
☐ _____	_____

Discussion Topics

☐ _____

☐ _____

☐ _____

☐ _____

☐ _____

☐ _____

☐ _____

Intentions & Goals

Notes

Show Rating: ☆☆☆☆☆

Episode Details

Title:

Episode #:

Recording Date: Release Date:

HOSTS	GUESTS

Hosts:
- ☐ _____
- ☐ _____
- ☐ _____

Guests:
- _____
- _____
- _____

Discussion Topics

- ☐ _____
- ☐ _____
- ☐ _____
- ☐ _____
- ☐ _____
- ☐ _____
- ☐ _____

Intentions & Goals

Notes

Show Rating: ☆ ☆ ☆ ☆ ☆

Episode Details

Title:

Episode #:

Recording Date: Release Date:

HOSTS	GUESTS
☐ _____	_____
☐ _____	_____
☐ _____	_____

Discussion Topics

☐ _____

☐ _____

☐ _____

☐ _____

☐ _____

☐ _____

☐ _____

Intentions & Goals

Notes

Show Rating: ☆☆☆☆☆

Episode Details

Title:

Episode #:

Recording Date: Release Date:

HOSTS	GUESTS
☐ _____	_____
☐ _____	_____
☐ _____	_____

Discussion Topics

☐ _____

☐ _____

☐ _____

☐ _____

☐ _____

☐ _____

☐ _____

Intentions & Goals

_____
_____
_____
_____

Notes

_____
_____
_____
_____
_____
_____
_____
_____
_____
_____
_____
_____
_____

Show Rating: ☆☆☆☆☆

Episode Details

Title:

Episode #:

Recording Date:

Release Date:

HOSTS	GUESTS

Discussion Topics

Intentions & Goals

_____
_____
_____

Notes

_____
_____
_____
_____
_____
_____
_____
_____
_____
_____
_____
_____

Show Rating: ☆☆☆☆☆

Episode Details

Title:

Episode #:

Recording Date: Release Date:

HOSTS	GUESTS

Discussion Topics

Intentions & Goals

_____
_____
_____

Notes

_____
_____
_____
_____
_____
_____
_____
_____
_____
_____
_____

Show Rating: ☆☆☆☆☆

Episode Details

Title:

Episode #:

Recording Date: _____   Release Date: _____

HOSTS	GUESTS

☐ _____   _____

☐ _____   _____

☐ _____   _____

Discussion Topics

☐ _____

☐ _____

☐ _____

☐ _____

☐ _____

☐ _____

☐ _____

Intentions & Goals

_____

_____

_____

_____

Notes

_____

_____

_____

_____

_____

_____

_____

_____

_____

_____

_____

_____

Show Rating: ☆☆☆☆☆

Episode Details

Title:

Episode #:

Recording Date: Release Date:

HOSTS	GUESTS

Discussion Topics

Intentions & Goals

_____

_____

_____

_____

Notes

_____

_____

_____

_____

_____

_____

_____

_____

_____

_____

_____

_____

Show Rating: ☆☆☆☆☆

Episode Details

Title:

Episode #:

Recording Date: Release Date:

HOSTS	GUESTS
☐ _____	_____
☐ _____	_____
☐ _____	_____

Discussion Topics

☐ _____

☐ _____

☐ _____

☐ _____

☐ _____

☐ _____

☐ _____

Intentions & Goals

_____

_____

_____

_____

Notes

_____

_____

_____

_____

_____

_____

_____

_____

_____

_____

_____

_____

Show Rating: ☆☆☆☆☆

Episode Details

Title:

Episode #:

Recording Date: Release Date:

HOSTS	GUESTS
☐ _____	_____
☐ _____	_____
☐ _____	_____

Discussion Topics

☐ _____

☐ _____

☐ _____

☐ _____

☐ _____

☐ _____

☐ _____

Intentions & Goals

Notes

Show Rating: ☆☆☆☆☆

Episode Details

Title:

Episode #:

Recording Date: Release Date:

HOSTS	GUESTS

Discussion Topics

Intentions & Goals

_____
_____
_____
_____

Notes

_____
_____
_____
_____
_____
_____
_____
_____
_____
_____
_____
_____

Show Rating: ☆☆☆☆☆

Episode Details

Title:

Episode #:

Recording Date: Release Date:

HOSTS	GUESTS

Discussion Topics

Intentions & Goals

Notes

Show Rating: ☆☆☆☆☆

Episode Details

Title:

Episode #:

Recording Date: Release Date:

HOSTS	GUESTS

Discussion Topics

Intentions & Goals

Notes

Show Rating: ☆ ☆ ☆ ☆ ☆

Episode Details

Title:

Episode #:

Recording Date: Release Date:

HOSTS	GUESTS

Discussion Topics

Intentions & Goals

_____

_____

_____

Notes

_____

_____

_____

_____

_____

_____

_____

_____

_____

_____

_____

Show Rating: ☆☆☆☆☆

Episode Details

Title:

Episode #:

Recording Date: Release Date:

HOSTS	GUESTS
☐ _____	_____
☐ _____	_____
☐ _____	_____

Discussion Topics

☐ _____

☐ _____

☐ _____

☐ _____

☐ _____

☐ _____

☐ _____

Intentions & Goals

_____

_____

_____

_____

Notes

_____

_____

_____

_____

_____

_____

_____

_____

_____

_____

_____

Show Rating: ☆☆☆☆☆

Episode Details

Title:

Episode #:

Recording Date: Release Date:

HOSTS	GUESTS

Hosts:
- _____
- _____
- _____

Guests:
- _____
- _____
- _____

Discussion Topics

- _____
- _____
- _____
- _____
- _____
- _____
- _____

Intentions & Goals

_____

_____

_____

Notes

_____

_____

_____

_____

_____

_____

_____

_____

_____

_____

_____

Show Rating: ☆☆☆☆☆

Episode Details

Title:

Episode #:

Recording Date: Release Date:

HOSTS	GUESTS

Discussion Topics

Intentions & Goals

_____

_____

_____

Notes

_____

_____

_____

_____

_____

_____

_____

_____

_____

_____

_____

_____

Show Rating: ☆☆☆☆☆

Episode Details

Title:

Episode #:

Recording Date: Release Date:

HOSTS	GUESTS

Discussion Topics

Intentions & Goals

Notes

Show Rating: ☆☆☆☆☆

Episode Details

Title:

Episode #:

Recording Date: Release Date:

HOSTS	GUESTS

Discussion Topics

Intentions & Goals

Notes

Show Rating: ☆☆☆☆☆

Episode Details

Title:

Episode #:

Recording Date: Release Date:

HOSTS	GUESTS

Discussion Topics

Intentions & Goals

_____

_____

_____

_____

Notes

_____

_____

_____

_____

_____

_____

_____

_____

_____

_____

_____

Show Rating: ☆☆☆☆☆

Episode Details

Title:

Episode #:

Recording Date: Release Date:

HOSTS	GUESTS

Discussion Topics

Intentions & Goals

_____
_____
_____
_____

Notes

_____
_____
_____
_____
_____
_____
_____
_____
_____
_____
_____
_____
_____

Show Rating: ☆ ☆ ☆ ☆ ☆

Episode Details

Title:

Episode #:

Recording Date: Release Date:

HOSTS	GUESTS

Discussion Topics

Intentions & Goals

Notes

Show Rating: ☆☆☆☆☆

Episode Details

Title:

Episode #:

Recording Date: Release Date:

HOSTS	GUESTS

Discussion Topics

Intentions & Goals

Notes

Show Rating: ☆☆☆☆☆

Episode Details

Title:

Episode #:

Recording Date: Release Date:

HOSTS	GUESTS

Discussion Topics

Intentions & Goals

Notes

Show Rating: ☆☆☆☆☆

Episode Details

Title:

Episode #:

Recording Date: Release Date:

HOSTS	GUESTS

Discussion Topics

Intentions & Goals

Notes

Show Rating: ☆ ☆ ☆ ☆ ☆

Episode Details

Title:

Episode #:

Recording Date: Release Date:

HOSTS	GUESTS

Discussion Topics

Intentions & Goals

_____

_____

_____

_____

Notes

_____

_____

_____

_____

_____

_____

_____

_____

_____

_____

_____

Show Rating: ☆☆☆☆☆

Episode Details

Title:

Episode #:

Recording Date: Release Date:

HOSTS	GUESTS
☐	
☐	
☐	

Discussion Topics

☐
☐
☐
☐
☐
☐
☐

Intentions & Goals

Notes

Show Rating: ☆ ☆ ☆ ☆ ☆

Episode Details

Title:

Episode #:

Recording Date: Release Date:

HOSTS	GUESTS
▢ _____	_____
▢ _____	_____
▢ _____	_____

Discussion Topics

▢ _____

▢ _____

▢ _____

▢ _____

▢ _____

▢ _____

▢ _____

Intentions & Goals

Notes

Show Rating: ☆☆☆☆☆

Episode Details

Title:

Episode #:

Recording Date: Release Date:

HOSTS	GUESTS

Discussion Topics

Intentions & Goals

Notes

Show Rating: ☆☆☆☆☆

Episode Details

Title:

Episode #:

Recording Date: Release Date:

HOSTS	GUESTS
☐ _____	_____
☐ _____	_____
☐ _____	_____

Discussion Topics

☐ _____

☐ _____

☐ _____

☐ _____

☐ _____

☐ _____

☐ _____

Intentions & Goals

_____

_____

_____

_____

Notes

_____

_____

_____

_____

_____

_____

_____

_____

_____

_____

_____

Show Rating: ☆☆☆☆☆

Episode Details

Title:

Episode #:

Recording Date: Release Date:

HOSTS	GUESTS
☐	
☐	
☐	

Discussion Topics

☐ _____

☐ _____

☐ _____

☐ _____

☐ _____

☐ _____

☐ _____

Intentions & Goals

Notes

Show Rating: ☆☆☆☆☆

Episode Details

Title:

Episode #:

Recording Date:　　　　　　　　Release Date:

HOSTS	GUESTS
☐ _____	_____
☐ _____	_____
☐ _____	_____

Discussion Topics

☐ _____

☐ _____

☐ _____

☐ _____

☐ _____

☐ _____

☐ _____

Intentions & Goals

_____

_____

_____

_____

Notes

_____

_____

_____

_____

_____

_____

_____

_____

_____

_____

_____

_____

Show Rating: ☆☆☆☆☆

Episode Details

Title:

Episode #:

Recording Date: Release Date:

HOSTS	GUESTS

Discussion Topics

Intentions & Goals

_____

_____

_____

Notes

_____

_____

_____

_____

_____

_____

_____

_____

_____

_____

_____

Show Rating: ☆☆☆☆☆

Episode Details

Title:

Episode #:

Recording Date: Release Date:

HOSTS	GUESTS

Discussion Topics

Intentions & Goals

Notes

Show Rating: ☆☆☆☆☆

Episode Details

Title:

Episode #:

Recording Date: Release Date:

HOSTS	GUESTS
☐ _____	_____
☐ _____	_____
☐ _____	_____

Discussion Topics

☐ _____

☐ _____

☐ _____

☐ _____

☐ _____

☐ _____

☐ _____

Intentions & Goals

Notes

Show Rating: ☆☆☆☆☆

Episode Details

Title:

Episode #:

Recording Date: Release Date:

HOSTS	GUESTS

Discussion Topics

Intentions & Goals

_____

_____

_____

_____

Notes

_____

_____

_____

_____

_____

_____

_____

_____

_____

_____

_____

Show Rating: ☆ ☆ ☆ ☆ ☆

Episode Details

Title:

Episode #:

Recording Date: Release Date:

HOSTS	GUESTS

Discussion Topics

Intentions & Goals

_____

_____

_____

_____

Notes

_____

_____

_____

_____

_____

_____

_____

_____

_____

_____

Show Rating: ☆☆☆☆☆

Episode Details

Title:

Episode #:

Recording Date: Release Date:

HOSTS	GUESTS

Discussion Topics

- _____
- _____
- _____
- _____
- _____
- _____
- _____

Intentions & Goals

_____

_____

_____

_____

Notes

_____

_____

_____

_____

_____

_____

_____

_____

_____

_____

_____

_____

_____

Show Rating: ☆ ☆ ☆ ☆ ☆

Episode Details

Title:

Episode #:

Recording Date:

Release Date:

HOSTS	GUESTS

Discussion Topics

Made in the USA
Coppell, TX
29 April 2022

77226669R00105